LOOKING BACK

THE PEOPLES OF
NORTH
AMERICA
BEFORE 1700

CHRISTINE HATT

EVANS BROTHERS LIMITED

Evans Brothers Limited
2A Portman Mansions
Chiltern Street
London W1M 1LE

First published 1998

British Library Cataloguing in Publication Data

Hatt, Christine
  The peoples of North America : before 1700. -
(Looking back)
  1. Indians of North America - History - Juvenile
literature
  I.Title
  970'.00497

ISBN 0237517280

Editor: Nicola Barber
Designer: Neil Sayer
Picture research: Victoria Brooker
Maps: Nick Hawken
Production: Jenny Mulvanny

Consultant: Dr Karen Harvey, Associate Dean,
University College, University of Denver

Printed in Spain by GRAFO, S.A. - Bilbao

Cover pictures:
(Main picture) Chaco Canyon, New Mexico
(Inset) A copper plaque from the Northwest
culture area

Acknowledgements

Cover (main image) Werner Forman Archive (background) Eye Ubiquitous **Title page** Seattle Art
Museum, Gift of John H. Hauberg/Paul Macapia **page 7** (left) Stephen J Krasemann/Bruce Coleman
Limited (right) Mr Jules Cowan/Bruce Coleman Limited **page 9** British Museum/Bridgeman Art
Library **page 12** (left) Werner Forman Archive (right) British Museum **page 13** Utah Museum of
Natural History **page 14** Salamander Picture Library **page 15** © 1996 Comstock, Inc **page 16** (top
and bottom) Werner Forman Archive **page 17** Werner Forman Archive **page 18** Werner Forman
Archive **page 20** (top) Werner Forman Archive (bottom) A.J.G. Bell/Eye Ubiquitous **page 21**
Richard A. Cooke/Corbis **page 22** Lynton Gardiner/© American Museum of Natural History **page
24** Peter Newark's Pictures **page 25** (top) Werner Forman Archive (bottom) Werner Forman
Archive **page 27** Werner Forman Archive **page 29** Library of Congress/Corbis **page 30** Gunter
Marx/Corbis **page 31** (top) Peter Newark's Western Americana (bottom) Lynton Gardiner/©
American Museum of Natural History **page 32** Museum of History and Industry/Corbis **page 33**
Library of Congress/Corbis **page 34** Werner Forman Archive **page 35** Peter Newark's Western
Americana **page 36** Michael Maslan Historic Photographs/Corbis **page 37** The National
Archives/Corbis **page 38** Phil Shermeister/© Corbis **page 39** Lynton Gardiner/© American
Museum of Natural History **page 40** Michael Maslan Historic Photographs/Corbis **page 41** Peter
Newark's Western Americana **page 42** Peter Newark's American Pictures **page 43** L.
Johnstone/Eye Ubiquitous **page 44** Seattle Art Museum, Gift of John H. Hauberg/Paul Macapia
page 46 Peter Newark's American Pictures **page 47** David Muench/Corbis **page 48** British
Museum/Bridgeman Art Library **page 49** (top) Lynton Gardiner/© American Museum of Natural
History (bottom) E. O. Hoppé/Corbis **page 51** Werner Forman Archive **page 52** Werner Forman
Archive **page 53** Salamander Picture Library **page 54** (bottom) Werner Forman Archive **page 55**
Peter Newark's American Pictures **page 57** Werner Forman Archive **page 59** Barry Davies/Eye
Ubiquitous

CONTENTS

INTRODUCTION

This book tells the story of the people who inhabited North America before the arrival of Europeans in the 16th century. It explains how people first reached North America many thousands of years ago, and how they gradually spread far and wide across the continent. It examines the extraordinary variety of life styles and forms of government they developed, as well as their complex spiritual beliefs. Finally, it looks briefly at the devastating impact of European arrival and colonisation on the native population up to 1700 and beyond.

A CLOSER LOOK

When the Italian explorer, Christopher Columbus, set sail from Spain in 1492, he was not looking for the Americas. In fact, he did not even know they existed. His aim was to find a sea route to Asia, as the Portuguese controlled the trade routes around Africa, and the overland journey from Europe to the East was long and dangerous. Columbus called his mission the 'Enterprise of the Indies', because one of the destinations he hoped to reach was India. When Columbus first arrived in the Americas, he assumed that he had achieved his goal. So he called the native peoples that he encountered 'Indians', but today they are more accurately known as Native Americans or American Indians. Columbus's voyages marked the beginning of European contact with the peoples of the Americas, and of the continent's transformation.

ENVIRONMENTS AND LIFE STYLES

North America is a huge landmass, covering about 23.5 million square kilometres. Within this vast area there are many different landscapes, from the frozen wastes of the Arctic north to the dry, dusty deserts of the southwest. When Europeans arrived, it is estimated that there were roughly seven million people living in North America, divided into more than 300 tribes. Each tribe had its own unique way of life, which depended largely on its particular environment.

To help them study and understand the Native Americans of North America, anthropologists have divided the continent into ten culture areas (see map

INTRODUCTION

Native Americans made – and continue to make – their homes in places as diverse as icy Baffin Island, Canada (left) and the arid deserts of Arizona, southwestern USA (below).

page 8). These are regions whose natural features (for example rivers, forests or mountains), climate, animals and plants greatly influenced the life styles of their Native American inhabitants. Within each culture area, many tribes shared food-finding methods, and often used the same locally available materials for building their homes.

Tribes within an area often differed from one another in important ways, too. In many areas, some tribes were nomadic, while others lived in permanent villages and towns. On the fringes of each area, tribes often had 'mixed' life styles. These included customs and practices that were typical of the neighbouring area, as well as of their own.

LANGUAGE FAMILES

Between them, 15th-century North Americans spoke more than 200 languages – perhaps as many as 600. Anthropologists have used these as another

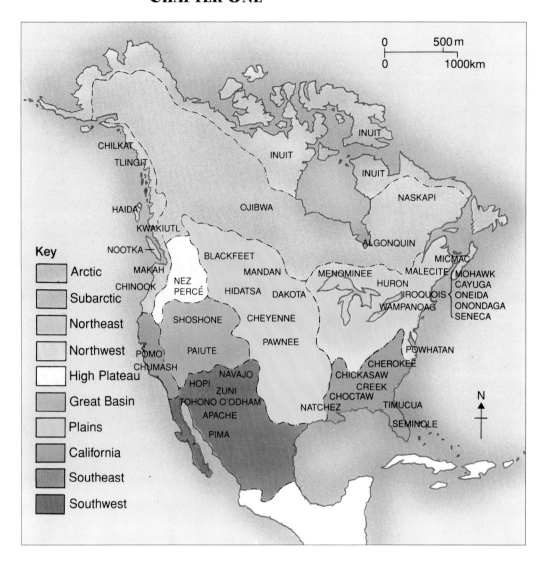

This map shows the ten culture areas into which modern anthropologists divide the North American continent.

way of dividing the tribes into groups for study, but language divisions have proved much harder to define than culture areas. This is partly because there is not enough evidence – none of the Native American languages of North America had a written form. However, most experts now agree that between 21 and 30 language families (groups of related languages) existed in North America at the time of European contact.

HOW DO WE KNOW?

The tribes of ancient North America kept no written records of any kind. This lack of written evidence

Introduction

The manner of their attire and painting them selues when they goe to their generall huntings or at theire Solemne feasts.

During the late 16th century, English explorer John White spent some time in the American Southeast. A talented artist, he compiled a sketchbook of the local Native Americans, including this image of a young warrior.

has hampered historians' efforts to piece together an accurate picture of life before the arrival of Europeans. But fortunately, other sources of information are available. Archaeologists working in many parts of the continent have unearthed a huge variety of objects, including tools, weapons, pottery, animal bones and food preparation equipment, such as stones for grinding seeds.

In some major archaeological sites, hundreds of objects have been discovered. In ancient burial grounds of the eastern woodlands, for example, there are human remains, and grave goods such as bracelets and pipes. In the buffalo and mammoth kill sites of the plains, there are mounds of animal bones, as well as weapons, and tools for carving meat from carcasses.

The lack of written evidence has forced historians to turn to the accounts of the first European explorers and settlers in North America for information about early Native American life. But they treat these sources with caution. Most Europeans of the period did not speak Native American languages, although they sometimes tried to communicate using sign language. As a result, they had little understanding of Native American ideas and beliefs, but simply recorded their assumptions as facts. Some Europeans were prejudiced against Native Americans, believing them to be uneducated savages. Others saw them only as slaves, potential converts to Christianity or sources of valuable trade goods. For all these reasons, 15th- and 16th-century European sources are often unreliable.

ARRIVAL AND SETTLEMENT

The landbridge that emerged between Siberia and Alaska during the last Ice Age allowed people to walk from Asia to North America. Avoiding the massive ice sheets that covered much of the continent, they then made their way south.

The first people ever to set foot on North American soil arrived there towards the end of the last Ice Age. At that time, so much of the world's water was frozen that the sea level fell by about 100 metres. As a result, large areas of land emerged from beneath the waves. In the far north, newly revealed land formed a bridge between Siberia in Asia, and Alaska in North America. This 1600-kilometre-wide landbridge, known as Beringia, provided the route for the earliest migrations into the Americas.

The first migrants from Asia did not set out to reach North America. They were simply bands of

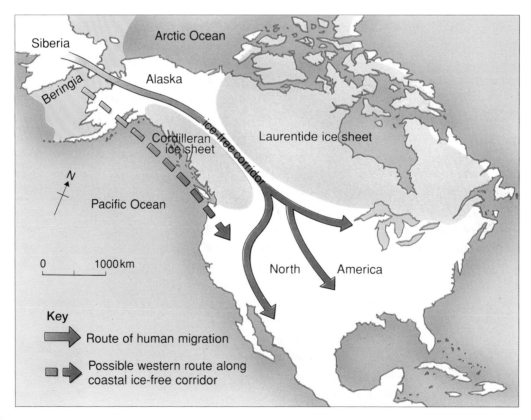

hunters who followed their prey of giant buffalo, mammoths, mastodons and other big game across Beringia and unknowingly entered a different continent. Then they gradually spread south, making their way along an ice-free corridor between the two vast ice sheets that covered much of the land. Some experts believe that there was a second ice-free route far to the west but this has yet to be proved.

A QUESTION OF TIME

Most experts agree that this was *how* people came to the Americas. But there are many opinions about exactly *when* they made their journeys. Beringia first emerged about 60,000 years ago, then disappeared and reappeared from time to time over the next 50,000 years, as the sea level rose and fell. To find out when people crossed this landbridge, archaeologists have measured the age of the most ancient camp sites and tools in the Americas using radiocarbon dating. The results were confusing. In Alaska, where the migrants probably arrived first, objects about 12,000 years old have been found. Further to the south, objects dating back about 14,000 years have been discovered. Even more strangely, in South America, far from Beringia, objects over 30,000 years old have been unearthed. The experts are still searching for more conclusive evidence. For now, they can only estimate that the peopling of the Americas occurred over many thousands of years, some time between 40,000 and 12,000 years ago.

THE PALAEO-INDIAN PERIOD

Archaeologists call the era of American history that lasted from the time of the first human settlements

A CLOSER LOOK

Clovis points were flaked on both sides and had a broad groove, known as a flute, rising about halfway up from their crescent-shaped bases. This was probably to make it easy for hunters to attach wooden spear shafts. Folsom points were usually smaller and more delicately flaked, with flutes extending all the way from the base to the top.

A Folsom point

A Clovis point

until about 10,000 years ago the Palaeo-Indian ('ancient Indian') Period. Palaeo-Indians are divided into cultures according to the type of stone tools they made. One of the most widespread was the Clovis culture, which lasted from about 10,000 to 9200 BC. It was named after Clovis, New Mexico. The people of the Clovis culture were nomadic hunters who lived on animals such as tapirs, small prehistoric horses, buffalo and especially mammoths. They killed and cut up their prey with Clovis points – spearheads and other tools produced by chipping flakes from pieces of flint. A slightly later Palaeo-Indian culture was the Folsom culture. Its members were big-game hunters, too, but their main prey was buffalo.

Although all Palaeo-Indians were big game hunters, they probably also ate plant foods such as berries, fruits and nuts. This method of obtaining food is called hunting and gathering, and it was used by early peoples not just in North America but all over the world.

THE ARCHAIC PERIOD

About 11,000 years ago, the Ice Age began to come to an end, the giant glaciers started to melt and temperatures gradually rose. This process of warming brought great changes to North America. First, the landscape altered. The band of evergreen forests and wide, treeless tundra that had covered the centre of the continent moved northwards with the ice. In its place, vast open grasslands, dry plains and deciduous forests appeared. At the same time, mammoths, mastodons and many other Ice Age mammals died out, probably as a result of the loss of their icy habitats.

The transformation of the landscape and climate made it essential for early North Americans to alter their way of life and adapt to the changing environment. They became less reliant on big game hunting and adopted a more varied range of hunter-gatherer life styles from about 8000 BC. This marked the beginning of the Archaic Period.

Archaic Indians spread across North America, settling in many regions that had previously been too inhospitable. Once they had chosen their territory, many became less nomadic. Some groups evolved a yearly route around a few fixed sites, such as lakesides or caves, while a few even settled in one area. This was only possible where food supplies were abundant, for example on the Northwest Coast, where fish, seabirds, berries and nuts were always available.

The Archaic Period came to an end when North Americans began to cultivate their own food – in other words, to farm. In some areas, such as the Northeast, this happened in about 1000 BC. But in others, such as the Northwest, people continued to hunt animals and gather plants until Europeans arrived and transformed their ancient ways of life.

Many objects from the Archaic Period have been unearthed in Danger Cave, which is located high above the Great Salt Lake in Utah. They include the remains of baskets and nets, as well as bone tools and stone spearheads like this one.

A CLOSER LOOK

As they adapted their skills to the new conditions, Archaic Indians produced many new tools and weapons. Unlike the Palaeo-Indians, who all used very similar implements, each Archaic group designed tools suitable for its own specific needs. In the Northeast woodlands, for example, people designed tools for hollowing out tree trunks to make canoes. Archaic tools were also made with a much wider range of materials, including copper, bone and clay, as well as stone.

EARLY CULTURES

A CLOSER LOOK
Early North Americans cultivated gourds and squash for their seeds and flesh, and some species of sunflower for their oil-filled seeds. Another type of sunflower was grown for its underground tubers (below). In English, these tubers are known as Jerusalem artichokes, a strange name that comes from the Italian word for sunflower, *girasole*.

The peoples of the North American cultures that emerged at the end of the Archaic Period grew crops such as gourds, squash and sunflowers (see box). At first, these foods made up only a minor part of their diet, which still largely consisted of meat, fish, wild berries, nuts and roots. But as Native Americans' farming skills improved, cultivated crops gradually became more important. As well as eating these foods immediately they were harvested, people also learned to store them. This allowed them to survive in times of drought, when wild plant foods and animals were not available.

Some Native Americans did not become farmers. In some places, such as along the Northwest Coast, people continued their lives as hunters and gatherers, relying on the plentiful supplies of wild food in these areas (see page 13).

THE ADENA CULTURE

The Adena people established one of the earliest cultures of this era, which is sometimes known as the Woodland Period. They lived in the eastern woodlands of the Ohio River valley from about 1000 BC, and left behind archaeological remains in over 200 sites. Many Adena settlements contained huge earthworks, often in the shape of squares or circles. But the most extraordinary of these

The extraordinary Great Serpent Mound in Ohio was first excavated in 1885. Many modern archaeologists think that it was built by the Adena people. Others believe that its impressive size and construction mark it out as the work of the more ambitious Hopewell (see page 16).

structures, the 217-metre-long Great Serpent Mound in Adams County, Ohio, takes the form of a giant snake. Experts believe that the Adena earthworks were probably used for religious rituals.

Many Adena villages had a second distinctive feature – massive earth burial mounds up to 20 metres high. The graves underneath these cone- and dome-shaped mounds were of two main types. Simple clay basins contained the cremated remains of ordinary people. More elaborate log tombs were the final resting places of the wealthy. The difference between the tombs of rich and poor shows that, unlike the earliest Americans, the Adena had developed a form of hierarchical society, probably ruled by clan chiefs.

The grave goods found inside these tombs have provided archaeologists with a great deal of evidence about the Adena way of life. Bracelets and spoons made of copper from Michigan, and beads made of shells from southern coasts, prove that the Adena had trade links with Native Americans in other parts of the continent. Tubular pipes suggest that they grew and smoked tobacco, probably as part of religious ceremonies.

CHAPTER THREE

THE HOPEWELL CULTURE

In about 300 BC, the Hopewell mound-building culture replaced the Adena in Ohio, then spread out in every direction. The Hopewell cultivated maize as well as the sunflowers and other crops of the Adena. At the same time, they continued to hunt game and gather the abundant wild plant foods in the region. This combination of agriculture, hunting and gathering led to an increase in population.

This vicious-looking bird claw was cut from mica by an artist of the Hopewell culture.

Everything the Adena had done, the Hopewell did on a grander scale. They constructed huge earthworks, some of which covered an area of 40 hectares. These structures were probably ceremonial centres where sacred rituals were carried out. High banks enclosed the earthworks and inside were numerous burial mounds, as well as the homes of religious leaders and the ruling clan chiefs. Outside were the farms of ordinary people, who lived in wigwams.

Excavations in the Hopewell tombs have unearthed a dazzling array of grave goods. They include jewellery, shapes cut from sheets of mica, carved tobacco

A CLOSER LOOK

Many other North American cultures were slowly evolving as those in the east and Southwest emerged. In the eastern Arctic, the Dorset culture arose in about 1000 BC. Its people made harpoons to catch walruses and seals, and built igloos and kayaks. In about AD 1000, the Thule culture developed in Alaska and spread east, finally taking over the Dorset people. The Thule were the ancestors of today's Inuit.

A bone-handled knife, made by a member of the Thule culture. The bone has been skilfully carved into the shape of a polar bear. Its head is clearly visible on the right.

THE PEOPLES OF
NORTH
AMERICA
BEFORE 1700

CHRISTINE HATT

EVANS BROTHERS LIMITED

Evans Brothers Limited
2A Portman Mansions
Chiltern Street
London W1M 1LE

First published 1998

British Library Cataloguing in Publication Data

Hatt, Christine
  The peoples of North America : before 1700. -
(Looking back)
  1. Indians of North America - History - Juvenile
literature
  I.Title
  970'.00497

ISBN 0237517280

Editor: Nicola Barber
Designer: Neil Sayer
Picture research: Victoria Brooker
Maps: Nick Hawken
Production: Jenny Mulvanny

Consultant: Dr Karen Harvey, Associate Dean,
University College, University of Denver

Printed in Spain by GRAFO, S.A. - Bilbao

Cover pictures:
(Main picture) Chaco Canyon, New Mexico
(Inset) A copper plaque from the Northwest
culture area

Acknowledgements

Cover (main image) Werner Forman Archive (background) Eye Ubiquitous **Title page** Seattle Art
Museum, Gift of John H. Hauberg/Paul Macapia **page 7** (left) Stephen J Krasemann/Bruce Coleman
Limited (right) Mr Jules Cowan/Bruce Coleman Limited **page 9** British Museum/Bridgeman Art
Library **page 12** (left) Werner Forman Archive (right) British Museum **page 13** Utah Museum of
Natural History **page 14** Salamander Picture Library **page 15** © 1996 Comstock, Inc **page 16** (top
and bottom) Werner Forman Archive **page 17** Werner Forman Archive **page 18** Werner Forman
Archive **page 20** (top) Werner Forman Archive (bottom) A.J.G. Bell/Eye Ubiquitous **page 21**
Richard A. Cooke/Corbis **page 22** Lynton Gardiner/© American Museum of Natural History **page
24** Peter Newark's Pictures **page 25** (top) Werner Forman Archive (bottom) Werner Forman
Archive **page 27** Werner Forman Archive **page 29** Library of Congress/Corbis **page 30** Gunter
Marx/Corbis **page 31** (top) Peter Newark's Western Americana (bottom) Lynton Gardiner/©
American Museum of Natural History **page 32** Museum of History and Industry/Corbis **page 33**
Library of Congress/Corbis **page 34** Werner Forman Archive **page 35** Peter Newark's Western
Americana **page 36** Michael Maslan Historic Photographs/Corbis **page 37** The National
Archives/Corbis **page 38** Phil Shermeister/© Corbis **page 39** Lynton Gardiner/© American
Museum of Natural History **page 40** Michael Maslan Historic Photographs/Corbis **page 41** Peter
Newark's Western Americana **page 42** Peter Newark's American Pictures **page 43** L.
Johnstone/Eye Ubiquitous **page 44** Seattle Art Museum, Gift of John H. Hauberg/Paul Macapia
page 46 Peter Newark's American Pictures **page 47** David Muench/Corbis **page 48** British
Museum/Bridgeman Art Library **page 49** (top) Lynton Gardiner/© American Museum of Natural
History (bottom) E. O. Hoppé/Corbis **page 51** Werner Forman Archive **page 52** Werner Forman
Archive **page 53** Salamander Picture Library **page 54** (bottom) Werner Forman Archive **page 55**
Peter Newark's American Pictures **page 57** Werner Forman Archive **page 59** Barry Davies/Eye
Ubiquitous

CONTENTS

INTRODUCTION

This book tells the story of the people who inhabited North America before the arrival of Europeans in the 16th century. It explains how people first reached North America many thousands of years ago, and how they gradually spread far and wide across the continent. It examines the extraordinary variety of life styles and forms of government they developed, as well as their complex spiritual beliefs. Finally, it looks briefly at the devastating impact of European arrival and colonisation on the native population up to 1700 and beyond.

A CLOSER LOOK

When the Italian explorer, Christopher Columbus, set sail from Spain in 1492, he was not looking for the Americas. In fact, he did not even know they existed. His aim was to find a sea route to Asia, as the Portuguese controlled the trade routes around Africa, and the overland journey from Europe to the East was long and dangerous. Columbus called his mission the 'Enterprise of the Indies', because one of the destinations he hoped to reach was India. When Columbus first arrived in the Americas, he assumed that he had achieved his goal. So he called the native peoples that he encountered 'Indians', but today they are more accurately known as Native Americans or American Indians. Columbus's voyages marked the beginning of European contact with the peoples of the Americas, and of the continent's transformation.

ENVIRONMENTS AND LIFE STYLES

North America is a huge landmass, covering about 23.5 million square kilometres. Within this vast area there are many different landscapes, from the frozen wastes of the Arctic north to the dry, dusty deserts of the southwest. When Europeans arrived, it is estimated that there were roughly seven million people living in North America, divided into more than 300 tribes. Each tribe had its own unique way of life, which depended largely on its particular environment.

To help them study and understand the Native Americans of North America, anthropologists have divided the continent into ten culture areas (see map

Introduction

Native Americans made – and continue to make – their homes in places as diverse as icy Baffin Island, Canada (left) and the arid deserts of Arizona, southwestern USA (below).

page 8). These are regions whose natural features (for example rivers, forests or mountains), climate, animals and plants greatly influenced the life styles of their Native American inhabitants. Within each culture area, many tribes shared food-finding methods, and often used the same locally available materials for building their homes.

Tribes within an area often differed from one another in important ways, too. In many areas, some tribes were nomadic, while others lived in permanent villages and towns. On the fringes of each area, tribes often had 'mixed' life styles. These included customs and practices that were typical of the neighbouring area, as well as of their own.

Language families

Between them, 15th-century North Americans spoke more than 200 languages – perhaps as many as 600. Anthropologists have used these as another

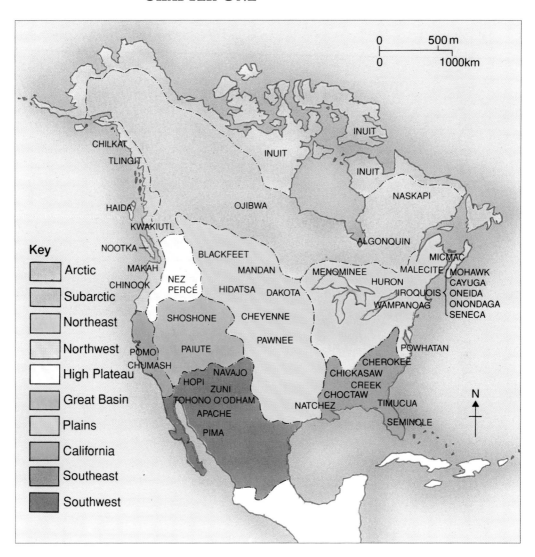

This map shows the ten culture areas into which modern anthropologists divide the North American continent.

Key

Arctic

Subarctic

Northeast

Northwest

High Plateau

Great Basin

Plains

California

Southeast

Southwest

way of dividing the tribes into groups for study, but language divisions have proved much harder to define than culture areas. This is partly because there is not enough evidence – none of the Native American languages of North America had a written form. However, most experts now agree that between 21 and 30 language families (groups of related languages) existed in North America at the time of European contact.

HOW DO WE KNOW?

The tribes of ancient North America kept no written records of any kind. This lack of written evidence

INTRODUCTION

The manner of their attire and painting themselves when they goe to their generall huntings, or at theire Solemne feasts.

During the late 16th century, English explorer John White spent some time in the American Southeast. A talented artist, he compiled a sketchbook of the local Native Americans, including this image of a young warrior.

has hampered historians' efforts to piece together an accurate picture of life before the arrival of Europeans. But fortunately, other sources of information are available. Archaeologists working in many parts of the continent have unearthed a huge variety of objects, including tools, weapons, pottery, animal bones and food preparation equipment, such as stones for grinding seeds.

In some major archaeological sites, hundreds of objects have been discovered. In ancient burial grounds of the eastern woodlands, for example, there are human remains, and grave goods such as bracelets and pipes. In the buffalo and mammoth kill sites of the plains, there are mounds of animal bones, as well as weapons, and tools for carving meat from carcasses.

The lack of written evidence has forced historians to turn to the accounts of the first European explorers and settlers in North America for information about early Native American life. But they treat these sources with caution. Most Europeans of the period did not speak Native American languages, although they sometimes tried to communicate using sign language. As a result, they had little understanding of Native American ideas and beliefs, but simply recorded their assumptions as facts. Some Europeans were prejudiced against Native Americans, believing them to be uneducated savages. Others saw them only as slaves, potential converts to Christianity or sources of valuable trade goods. For all these reasons, 15th- and 16th-century European sources are often unreliable.

ARRIVAL AND SETTLEMENT

The landbridge that emerged between Siberia and Alaska during the last Ice Age allowed people to walk from Asia to North America. Avoiding the massive ice sheets that covered much of the continent, they then made their way south.

The first people ever to set foot on North American soil arrived there towards the end of the last Ice Age. At that time, so much of the world's water was frozen that the sea level fell by about 100 metres. As a result, large areas of land emerged from beneath the waves. In the far north, newly revealed land formed a bridge between Siberia in Asia, and Alaska in North America. This 1600-kilometre-wide landbridge, known as Beringia, provided the route for the earliest migrations into the Americas.

The first migrants from Asia did not set out to reach North America. They were simply bands of

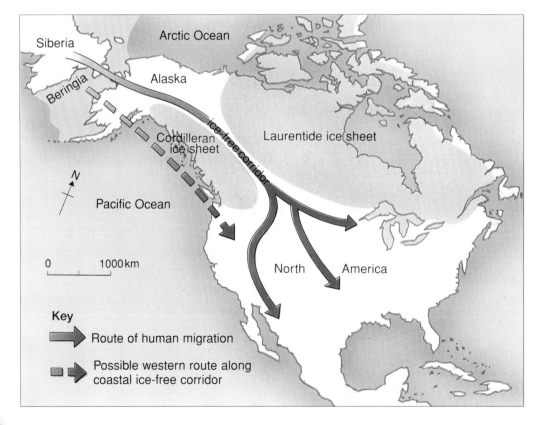

Siberia

Arctic Ocean

Beringia

Alaska

Cordilleran ice sheet

ice-free corridor

Laurentide ice sheet

N

Pacific Ocean

North America

0   1000 km

Key

Route of human migration

Possible western route along coastal ice-free corridor

The extraordinary Great Serpent Mound in Ohio was first excavated in 1885. Many modern archaeologists think that it was built by the Adena people. Others believe that its impressive size and construction mark it out as the work of the more ambitious Hopewell (see page 16).

structures, the 217-metre-long Great Serpent Mound in Adams County, Ohio, takes the form of a giant snake. Experts believe that the Adena earthworks were probably used for religious rituals.

Many Adena villages had a second distinctive feature – massive earth burial mounds up to 20 metres high. The graves underneath these cone- and dome-shaped mounds were of two main types. Simple clay basins contained the cremated remains of ordinary people. More elaborate log tombs were the final resting places of the wealthy. The difference between the tombs of rich and poor shows that, unlike the earliest Americans, the Adena had developed a form of hierarchical society, probably ruled by clan chiefs.

The grave goods found inside these tombs have provided archaeologists with a great deal of evidence about the Adena way of life. Bracelets and spoons made of copper from Michigan, and beads made of shells from southern coasts, prove that the Adena had trade links with Native Americans in other parts of the continent. Tubular pipes suggest that they grew and smoked tobacco, probably as part of religious ceremonies.

THE HOPEWELL CULTURE

In about 300 BC, the Hopewell mound-building culture replaced the Adena in Ohio, then spread out in every direction. The Hopewell cultivated maize as well as the sunflowers and other crops of the Adena. At the same time, they continued to hunt game and gather the abundant wild plant foods in the region. This combination of agriculture, hunting and gathering led to an increase in population.

This vicious-looking bird claw was cut from mica by an artist of the Hopewell culture.

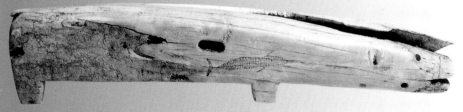

Everything the Adena had done, the Hopewell did on a grander scale. They constructed huge earthworks, some of which covered an area of 40 hectares. These structures were probably ceremonial centres where sacred rituals were carried out. High banks enclosed the earthworks and inside were numerous burial mounds, as well as the homes of religious leaders and the ruling clan chiefs. Outside were the farms of ordinary people, who lived in wigwams.

Excavations in the Hopewell tombs have unearthed a dazzling array of grave goods. They include jewellery, shapes cut from sheets of mica, carved tobacco

A CLOSER LOOK

Many other North American cultures were slowly evolving as those in the east and Southwest emerged. In the eastern Arctic, the Dorset culture arose in about 1000 BC. Its people made harpoons to catch walruses and seals, and built igloos and kayaks. In about AD 1000, the Thule culture developed in Alaska and spread east, finally taking over the Dorset people. The Thule were the ancestors of today's Inuit.

A bone-handled knife, made by a member of the Thule culture. The bone has been skilfully carved into the shape of a polar bear. Its head is clearly visible on the right.

People of the Natchez tribe carry their ruler, the Great Sun, to a harvest celebration.

NORTHEASTERN SOCIETY

Tribes in the Northeast were divided into clans, each with its own animal symbol, such as a deer, beaver or wolf. All the members of a clan believed that they were descended from the same ancestors. Marriage was only permitted between a man and a woman of different clans, and a new husband often went to live with his wife's family. If the woman later wanted a divorce, she simply put her husband's possessions outside the door of their multi-family longhouse. Children were named by their mothers, and usually inherited membership of their mother's clan.

The method of government practised in the Northeast relied on everyone working together for the good of the entire community. Each clan had its own chief. If a decision had to be made that would affect the whole tribe, these men (or occasionally women) met to come to a decision. Any family or clan that disagreed was free to move away.

A CLOSER LOOK

The Iroquois tribes of the Northeast were often at war with one another and with the other major group of tribes in the region, the Algonquians. But during the late 16th century, possibly before contact with Europeans had occurred, the Mohawk, Onondaga, Seneca, Oneida and Cayuga tribes joined together to form the Iroquois League. This was essentially a political alliance designed to end the violence between them and to strengthen their position in relation to other tribes.

FINDING FOOD

Native Americans obtained food in many ways. In some areas, such as the Northwest, tribes continued the hunter-gatherer life style of the Archaic Period (see page 13) until the arrival of Europeans. In the Southeast and Northeast, the Southwest and parts of the Great Plains, naturally available food supplies were supplemented by agricultural produce. In barren areas such as the Great Basin, people lived by foraging for plant foods and trapping small animals.

LAND OF PLENTY

This patterned Tlingit basket was woven from spruce tree roots. Women used it for collecting berries.

The Northwest culture area was like a giant natural larder, with food almost everywhere. In the Pacific Ocean there were seals, sea lions, and whales. On the shoreline, there was a rich variety of shellfish. Rivers were bursting with salmon, herrings and sardines, as well as the oolakon fish, which provided a delicious oil used in cooking. Men caught these fish with spears, nets and rakes. They also trapped them behind small dams called weirs. Some of the Northwestern tribes were based too far inland to rely on the sea for food, so people from these tribes hunted bears, elks and mountain goats.

Throughout the area, women gathered many different plant foods, including blackberries and cranberries. They were also responsible for preparing and

FINDING FOOD

A Nootka whale hunter

cooking food. Meat and fish were often smoked, and fruits dried in the sun, to preserve them for future use.

FOOD FROM THE FREEZER

Finding food in the icy landscapes of the Arctic posed special problems. The lives of the Inuit followed an unchanging seasonal cycle. In winter, they built igloos on the frozen sea, hunted walruses and seals, and fished through holes in the ice with pronged spears. As spring slowly returned, they moved inland to catch lake fish and pick crowberries, sorrel and other plants. Summer was the time for hunting seals, whales and other sea mammals in the newly melted coastal waters. The Inuit pursued seals in light canoes called kayaks. To chase larger prey they preferred bigger sailing boats,

This umiak set sail from Grantley Harbor in Alaska in about 1904. However, the design of these boats has changed little over the centuries.

known as umiaks. As the summer ended, Inuit tracked lumbering herds of caribou and musk oxen as they migrated south for winter, killing them with spears, bows and arrows.

HUNTING THE BUFFALO

Two ways of life existed side-by-side in the Great Plains before the arrival of Europeans. Tribes such as the Mandan, Hidatsa and Pawnee lived in permanent river-valley villages. The women of these tribes were farmers, growing melons and sunflowers as well as maize, beans and squash. The men were hunters. Other tribes, such as the Blackfeet, were nomadic hunter-gatherers, following buffalo across the Plains all year round and collecting plant foods. Over the centuries, the numbers of these buffalo hunters swelled as other tribes arrived, forced from their homelands by enemy tribes or by Europeans.

The buffalo hunt was central to the Plains way of life. At the beginning of a hunt, shamans often tried to attract the animals by calling to their spirits and waving buffalo-shaped stones called *iniskims*. Then they left the hunters to catch their prey. In the years before Europeans brought horses to the Americas, a common method was to stampede a herd of buffalos over the edge of a cliff, so that the animals fell to their deaths below. Another technique was to put up a corral, then drive the animals into it.

A CLOSER LOOK

Plains women prepared buffalo meat for eating in many ways. They roasted huge joints over fires, and used scraps and bones to make stews and flavoured soups. Another favourite dish was pemmican. This was made by pounding strips of dried, salted buffalo meat into a powder, then mixing it with melted buffalo fat, dried berries and sometimes maple syrup. The paste was then rolled into balls, which were sweet, full of energy and longer-lasting than raw meat.

VARIED DIET

In the Southeast, people were both farmers and hunter-gatherers. A huge variety of crops flourished in the area's fertile lands, but the most important was maize. Both men and women worked in the fields, but carried out different tasks. In spring, men turned over the ground with hoes. Women followed behind, planting seeds. In summer, women tended the fields while men went hunting. In autumn, everyone harvested the crops and took part in the Green Corn Ceremony (see page 27).

A CLOSER LOOK

Fishermen from Southeastern tribes did not always rely on their skill with nets and spears alone. Sometimes they drugged fish by putting narcotic herbs into the rivers. Then they simply scooped the dazed creatures up from the surface of the water. The region's rivers and coasts provided the fishermen with other prey, too, including alligators and turtles.

This picture by John White (see page 9) shows Native Americans from North Carolina using many different methods to catch fish.

Agriculture was central to the Southeastern way of life, but hunting and fishing provided over a third of the population's food. Gathering was important, too – wild plant foods such as strawberries and peanuts made a major contribution to the varied diet of the Southeastern tribes.

FARMING AND FISHING

In the Northeast, tribes practised a combination of farming, gathering and hunting. The major crops were maize, beans and squash, but sunflowers and tobacco were also grown. Women carried out the bulk of the farm work, but it was the men's duty to prepare the fields for planting in spring by burning down shrubs and trees. Women also gathered fruits such as blueberries, raspberries and chokecherries. In the north of the area, around the Great Lakes, the most important wild plant food was wild rice.

The men of the Northeast hunted an amazing range of animals using bows, arrows and clubs. In the forests of the far north, moose, caribou and bears were important prey for tribes such as the Micmac and Malecite. The fishing in the Northeast was just as varied as the hunting. In spring, men

Many years ago, members of the Great Lakes tribes harvested wild rice in the early autumn. Sitting or standing in their birchbark canoes, they struck the plant stalks with sticks until the grains fell into their boats. These present-day Americans are using much the same technique.

netted young salmon as they hurled themselves up waterfalls towards their spawning grounds. In winter, they made holes in the ice and lowered hooks and lines to catch their prey.

DESERT AGRICULTURE

The Pueblo peoples of the Southwest grew onions, chilis and tomatoes, as well as maize, squash and beans. They also bred turkeys. As the climate was so dry, the tribes developed special techniques to make farming possible. They planted seeds deep in the earth so that they could tap into underground water, and diverted rivers on to the arid soil.

FORAGING FOR FOOD

In the deserts of the Great Basin there was so little rainfall that farming was impossible. Neither was there enough game for people to be full-time hunters, although they occasionally caught a few ducks, deer and rabbits. Instead they moved around the area foraging for berries, seeds and nuts, and catching small animals such as grasshoppers, lizards and prairie dogs.

Conditions in the more northerly High Plateau were less harsh. There, the Nez Percé and other tribes were able to catch salmon in the Columbia, Fraser and Snake rivers, and hunt deer and bighorn sheep. But they also foraged for camas bulbs, roots and other plant foods. The California culture area was more hospitable still, containing a wide range of environments from forests to coasts. More than 50 tribes lived there, each with its own specialised diet of local foods. However, despite the fertile land in much of the area, agriculture never developed.

Duck decoys like this were made from rushes by the Paiute Indians of the Great Basin. Placed on the water, they encouraged real ducks to land. The birds were then promptly caught by waiting hunters.

EVERYDAY LIFE

The housing, clothing and transport methods of the many North American tribes were just as varied as their means of finding food. Produced from the different materials available in the different culture areas, they made everyday life in each one distinct from that of its neighbours.

This Inuit couple from Alaska are dressed in fur clothes to keep out the bitter cold of the Arctic.

IGLOOS AND ANORAKS

The ingenious Inuit learned to make housing, clothing and canoes from the meagre resources available in their frozen lands. Igloos were built on thick sea ice during the winter hunting season (see pages 35-6). They were constructed from blocks of snow sawn out of the ground and shaped with snow knives. In spring and summer the Inuit made houses from other materials. In places where there was a supply of wood, such as Alaska, people used it to make a framework on which to spread animal skins or turf. Elsewhere, they made their houses from tightly packed turf and stones.

In the Arctic, protective clothing was essential for survival, so the Inuit covered themselves from head to toe in waterproof hooded anoraks, trousers and boots. The clothes were often made from caribou fur and the boots from sealskin. To shield their eyes from the reflection of the sun off brilliant white snow, the Inuit also wore wood or walrus-tusk goggles.

The people of the Arctic built lightweight kayaks by making driftwood frames then stretching sealskins across them. Sturdier umiaks (see page 36) were made from wood or whalebone frames covered in walrus hides. Hunters waterproofed both skins and hides by soaking them in seal oil. To travel overland, Inuit used wooden sleds drawn by huskies.

TENTS AND TOBOGGANS

Most Subarctic tribes, for example the Ojibwa, lived in wigwams. These were cone-shaped tents made from a framework of saplings with sheets of birchbark laid over the top. Wigwams were ideal for the tribes' nomadic way of life as they could be put up and taken down quickly and easily.

Winters in the Subarctic were long and severe, so its people favoured clothes made of caribou fur. On their feet they wore soft deerskin moccasins, but in the winter they sometimes bound snowshoes over the top. These were made from thin strips of caribou

To thank the Great Spirit for the first snowfall of winter, members of the Subarctic Ojibwa tribe perform the Snowshoe Dance.

hide woven into a mesh across a birchbark frame. They allowed their wearers to glide across the snow.

The Subarctic tribes depended on two main forms of transport, the birchbark canoe, which they had in common with the Northeastern peoples (see page 43), and the wooden toboggan, which was unique to them. Toboggans were made from planks mounted on curved runners that cut through the snow. The wood of the runners had to be softened in steam before it could be bent into the right shape. The toboggans were usually pulled by men.

BIRCHBARK BUILDERS

Northeastern peoples constructed a variety of houses. Many lived in wigwams, which were either cone- or dome-shaped. Some tribes covered the wooden frames of their wigwams with birchbark, but others used different materials. For example, the Menominee of the Great Lakes used woven mats of reeds.

The other distinctive dwelling of the region was the longhouse, in which the Iroquois and several

These Native Americans have erected their birchbark wigwams on the shores of Lake Huron, in present-day Canada.

EVERYDAY LIFE

other tribes lived. A longhouse was a rectangular structure up to 45 metres long. It was made by erecting a framework of wooden poles, tying them together with leather strips, then covering them with bark. Every longhouse was home to as many as 12 families, each of which occupied its own separate compartment, complete with raised sleeping platform. Food, utensils and clothes were stored on higher platforms, and a corridor ran down the centre where fires were built for cooking. Iroquois villages generally consisted of several, regularly spaced rows of longhouses surrounded by a stockade.

Northeastern tribes paddled around the rivers of their homelands in canoes. These graceful boats were made from sheets of birchbark stretched over cedarwood frames and waterproofed with the resin

A CLOSER LOOK

The typical clothing of the Northeast was made from the skins of animals such as deer and moose, sewn together with leather strips. Men wore jackets and leggings in winter and loincloths in summer, while women favoured belted, knee-length dresses. Deerskin moccasins were worn on the feet, sometimes in bootlike styles that came almost to the knee. Both clothes and shoes were often decorated with dyed porcupine quills.

This is a reconstruction of a longhouse built by members of the Huron tribe, who lived between Lake Huron and Lake Ontario.

of black spruce trees. The river systems of the Northeast were so complex that it was often quicker to cross from one river to another on foot than to make an entire journey by boat. Luckily, birchbark canoes were so light that they could easily be carried by one person.

The most striking garments in the Northwest were made by the Chilkat, a tribe of the Tlingit people. Their ceremonial shirts were woven from cedar bark and goat wool, and covered in designs based on family totems. The totem used in this shirt design is a bear.

LAND OF THE CEDAR

Much of the land along the Northwest Pacific coast was covered in dense cedar-tree forests. Northwestern tribes used the water-resistant wood from the trees for their houses. The style of Northwestern houses varied from region to region, but all of them had a fixed inner framework and a portable outer framework that could be replaced if necessary. Cedarwood was also used for chests, benches and other furniture inside the houses, and for cooking and storage boxes.

Northwestern tribes made many of their clothes from the bark of the cedar tree. In late spring every year, they pulled long strips of the bark from tree trunks. Then women wove these into clothes – bark blankets for men, bark skirts and cloaks for themselves – on upright looms. Clothes were also made from dog hair, mountain goat wool and sea otter fur.

Northwestern people used hollowed-out cedar logs to make their main means of transport – canoes. They built several types. Small, light canoes were made for shallow coastal and river waters, while for long ocean journeys, heavier vessels were constructed from massive tree trunks. Some large canoes were carved and painted with animal designs and used for special occasions such as weddings and potlatches (see page 31).

EVERYDAY LIFE

TIPIS AND TRAVOIS

The nomadic, hunting tribes of the Great Plains lived in tipis. These were cone-shaped tents made from painted buffalo hides stretched over a frame of pinewood poles. The lower half of each tipi was lined with a decorated dew cloth, which helped to keep it warm and dry inside. A fire for cooking and heating burned in the centre, and smoke escaped through a hole in the roof. Family tipis were about four metres wide, but much larger versions were erected for religious ceremonies and council meetings. All tipis were made and owned by women.

The farming tribes of the Plains lived in dome-shaped earth lodges sunk about a metre below ground. These were made from layers of wood, grass and earth resting on a central framework of tree trunks. From the outside they looked like giant molehills, with only an entranceway and smokehole betraying the fact that people – and animals – were living inside.

Most Plains clothing was made from deerskin, often decorated with porcupine quills. Everyday garments were similar across the region – loose shirts and leggings for men, straight shift dresses or skirts for women. However, ceremonial headdresses

The Plateau tribe known as the Nez Percé became expert horse breeders and traders after the arrival of Europeans. But here they are still using a dog-drawn travois.

and robes were more varied. For example, the eagle feather war bonnets of the Dakota hung down their backs to the ground, while those of Blackfeet warriors looked like crowns, with feathers pointing up towards the sky.

The nomadic peoples of the Plains transported their tipis and other goods on wooden frames called travois. A travois was made by joining two pinewood poles at one end to form a triangular shape, then slinging buffalo hides between the poles. Before Europeans arrived, dogs were used to pull travois, but later bigger, stronger horses took their place.

People of the settled Mandan tribe paddled small bullboats along the rivers of their homelands. They made these boats by creating a cup-shaped framework of flexible willow wood, then covering it with buffalo skins. Finished boats were gently heated while a mixture of buffalo fat and resin was rubbed into the joins between the hides to seal them.

DESERT DWELLERS

The Pueblo peoples of the Southwest lived in multistorey apartment houses made of adobe or stone (see page 21). However, Navajo and Apache homes were completely different. During the summer hunting season, when they moved frequently from place to place, these tribes built temporary shelters from branches and twigs. In the winter they constructed hogans – small, one-roomed structures consisting of cedar log frameworks covered with packed earth. If a person died inside a hogan, a hole was made in the wall to let their spirit out, and the house was never used again.

In the heat of the Southwestern pueblos there was no need for animal-skin garments. Instead clothes were made from cotton that had been spun and woven into fabric by men. As this cloth was naturally pale, colour was often added by applying vivid vegetable dyes. Pueblo women wore long dresses, which they fastened on the right shoulder, while men favoured shirts and leggings.

This earth-covered hogan is dwarfed by the spectacular scenery of Monument Valley, Arizona.

When the Apache and Navajo arrived in the Southwest during the 15th century, they wore skin garments. But they gradually began to barter for cotton clothing from the pueblos, and to spin and weave for themselves. However, it was not until after the arrival of the Spanish that they became skilled wool weavers. This tradition continues today (see page 53).

SOUTHEASTERN STYLE

Houses in the Southeast were extremely varied, although most were made from some combination of wood, bark, reeds and mud. The Natchez lived in domed, wood-framed huts with mud walls and thatched roofs. The Creek made two types of wooden, reed-roofed homes – open-sided summer houses and enclosed winter lodges insulated with clay. In every village they also built a large, circular building, used for

CHAPTER SEVEN

The Southeastern village of Pomeioc, Virginia, was also painted by John White (see page 9). Its houses were made of bark, reeds and wood.

council meetings and festivals, and a granary, used for storing corn. The village was often surrounded with a stockade or moat to keep hostile tribes out.

For much of the year, very little clothing was necessary in the humid southern half of the Southeast. Among tribes such as the Timucua of Florida men wore simple loincloths, while women favoured short, fringed skirts. These garments were usually made from coarsely woven cotton cloth. In the cooler northern half of the region, leather and fur were the most common clothing materials. But although clothes in the Southeast were simple, tattooing, jewellery, feather headdresses and elaborate hairstyles added variety and colour to the appearance of the different tribes.

WESTERN WAYS

The tribes of the Great Basin in western North America often lived in caves during the winter. In summer, as they moved around foraging for food, they built wickiups. These were small, conical dwellings made from a wooden framework covered with a layer of brush. The tribes of the more northerly High Plateau lived in circular pit houses during winter and in communal reed lodges in

EVERYDAY LIFE

After Europeans arrived in the Great Basin, local tribes developed new types of clothing. This jacket is decorated with European glass beads (see page 54).

summer. Clothes worn in both areas were simple – loincloths for men and apronlike garments for women – and usually made from animal skins or bark.

In general, the Native Americans of the Californian tribes wore little, as the heat of the region made clothing superfluous. Homes were of several types. Some tribes built small wickiups like those in the Great Basin. The coastal Pomo and Chumash tribes constructed thatched houses with wooden frames. But those of the Pomo were long and straight, while those of the Chumash were circular and domed. The Chumash were also remarkable for their boat-building skills. They made sturdy, seagoing canoes from pinewood. Other Californian tribes used tule reeds to make lighter boats for use on lakes and rivers.

A CLOSER LOOK

In the 18th century, a group of Native Americans from the Southeastern Creek tribe left their homes in the north of the region and went to Florida. These people became the Seminole (meaning 'breakaway') tribe and developed their own unique way of life among the swamps and lakes of the Everglades. They lived in open-sided, thatched houses on stilts called chickees, and wore multi-coloured cotton clothes. A strong Seminole community of about 14,000 people still exists today, evidence of the tribe's remarkable adaptability through changing times.

These two Seminole girls are wearing the traditional cotton costume of their tribe.

NORTH AMERICAN ARTS

For Native Americans, the ability to create a tool, or weave a garment, was seen as a special and important gift. For this reason, making and using beautiful and practical objects was an integral part of everyday life. It was one of the many ways in which they expressed their links with the world of the spirits and offered thanks to their gods. They generally worked with locally available materials, but trade networks, especially in the Southwest and Northwest, sometimes made it possible to use metals, shells and stones imported from elsewhere.

ARCTIC ART

The Inuit people were expert carvers of walrus ivory, wood and stone. Among the objects they most commonly produced were tiny carved figures, many of which have been unearthed in ancient Inuit sites. The exact purpose of these figures is unknown, but they may be charms used by shamans when they tried to contact Sedna (see page 26) and other gods.

The tribes of the Subarctic made ceremonial masks, some of them adorned with caribou fur. People of these tribes took great pride in the decoration of their clothes. Some used porcupine quills to create their designs, but the Naskapi tribe were famous for the red patterns they painted on their fur and skin garments.

A CLOSER LOOK
The Inuit carved elaborate masks, some with moving parts, for use in dances and spiritual ceremonies. These usually represented spirits or animals whose behaviour they hoped to influence through their rituals. Only men put on the full-size masks, while women wore miniature versions on their fingers. The Inuit also made a wide variety of everyday items, from canoe paddles to sun hats, which were carved or painted with ornate designs.

BASKETS, BOARDS AND BELTS

Not only did the Northeastern tribes use birchbark for wigwams and canoes, they also wove strips of this light, flexible material into baskets and boxes. These were often decorated with quills. Wood was carved to make other everyday objects, such as bowls, spoons and cradleboards for carrying babies.

The most distinctive objects made by the Iroquois tribes of the Northeast were wampum belts. These were long, broad bands of black, white and purple beads (wampum) made from whelk and clam shells. People gave one another gifts of wampum belts to mark important occasions such as marriages or peace agreements. They were sacred objects, and extremely valuable. Their patterns recorded important events from a tribe's history, and some men, known as Keepers of the Wampum, were specially trained to interpret them and recount the stories they told.

This beautifully shaped hat, decorated with a mountain goat crest, was woven from spruce tree roots by a member of the Haida tribe.

WOODWORK AND WEAVING

The people of the Northwestern tribes were skilled at carving and painting the wooden totem poles that stood in their villages and the masks that they wore at religious ceremonies (see page 25). They also carved a wide range of everyday objects, such as bowls, from other materials including stone, bone, antler and the twisted horns of mountain sheep. Many of the Northwestern peoples were expert weavers. Each of the bark and hair blankets woven by the Chilkat was unique (see page 44). Other tribes excelled at basketry. The Nootka and Haida, for example, wove spruce tree roots into hats and strips of cedar bark into baskets. To add colour, they stained grasses with fruit and plant dyes, then wove them into the finished basketwork.

PLAINS PAINTING

The creative skills of the nomadic Plains tribes were displayed for all to see on their tipis. Each family designed and painted its own tipi. Some chose to show events from their lives, such as hunting scenes or battles, while others preferred symbols intended to ward off evil. Geometric designs were also painted on to carrying cases called parfleches.

The people of the Plains excelled at quill and featherwork. Dyed porcupine quills were used to decorate everything from cradleboards to quivers. The feathers of golden eagles and other birds of prey were used for war bonnets and shields. Golden eagles were considered sacred, so men were not allowed to shoot them with arrows. Instead they had to kill them with their bare hands before plucking out the feathers.

Women of the Plains tribes made parfleches by folding buffalo hides. This parfleche was used to carry dried buffalo meat.

These Plains moccasins are finely decorated with porcupine quills.

PUEBLO POTTERY

Pottery was made from the earliest times in the Southwestern Pueblos, and at the time of European invasion in the 16th century it was still a widespread – and exclusively female – skill. Women made pots by coiling a roll of clay higher and higher, then rubbing the surface until the joins between the layers were smoothed away. They then painted the finished pots in the traditional colours of red, black and white. Some pots were used for everyday purposes such as storing food and water, but others played a part in sacred ceremonies. Zuni prayer bowls, for example, were filled with cornmeal then carried during rituals designed to bring rain.

The Pueblo peoples were expert weavers, producing garments from cotton, and baskets from plants such as reeds. They were also skilled

A CLOSER LOOK

The Apache and Navajo learned many of their skills from the Pueblo peoples, only developing their own distinctive wool-weaving techniques after contact with Europeans. During religious rituals, the Navajo also made sand paintings. These were pictures of the spirits made from sand, cornmeal, pollen and charcoal, and designed to encourage the spirits to do what the people wanted, for example cure the sick.

Navajo weavers at work

CHAPTER EIGHT

woodworkers and creative jewellers. They could paint, too, decorating the walls of their underground kivas with sacred and secret images.

SOUTHEASTERN SKILLS

One of the main crafts of the Southeast was basketry. Women from tribes such as the Cherokee dyed reed canes a variety of different colours, then wove them into baskets featuring geometric patterns. Women also made clay pots that were not painted, but covered in surface indentations. These were created by carving the design required on to a small wooden tool, then pressing this repeatedly over the pots.

A colourful Pomo basket, with hummingbird and other feathers worked into the weave.

WESTERN ARTS

In the Great Basin and the High Plateau, basketry was developed to a high level. Intricately woven baskets featuring complex designs and several colours were produced in many different styles. Among the most common were large, cone-shaped containers used for carrying plant foods. But it was the Pomo of California who were the supreme basketmakers of the west. They often used several materials, such as reeds, roots and bark, to form the basic framework of a basket, then wove hummingbird and other feathers into the design. The results were both stunning and unique.

THE ARRIVAL OF EUROPEANS

Christopher Columbus never set foot on North American soil. On the four voyages he made between 1492 and 1504, he visited only some Caribbean islands and the coasts of South and Central America. Nevertheless, his arrival was a major turning point in world history, and opened the way for Europeans to explore – and colonise – all the Americas. These lands were never to be the same again.

SPANISH ENCOUNTERS

It was the Spanish who made the first major explorations of North America, looking for gold and whatever else might make them rich. Between 1539 and 1542, Hernando de Soto and his men covered a vast area of the Southeast, beginning in what is now Florida and continuing as far as Texas. His treatment of the Native Americans was a sign of what was to come in many other parts of the continent. As he passed from one settlement to the next, he required

This 16th-century illustration shows Native Americans of Florida preparing a feast. Hernando de Soto would have witnessed scenes such as this as he made his way across the Southeast.

people to submit to him and convert to Christianity. If they refused to do so, he stole their goods, put them in chains and made them slaves. A similar story unfolded when Francisco Vásquez de Coronado encountered the Pueblo peoples of the Southwest in 1542.

The Spanish eventually colonised Florida in 1565. By 1700 they controlled much of the Southwest and were attempting to spread their way of life among its inhabitants. Their efforts to continue further up the west coast were hampered by Russians, who also laid claim to the land.

FRENCH EXPLORATION

Further north, it was the French who began to venture inland and meet Native American tribes. Frenchman Jacques Cartier arrived in Canada in 1534 and made his final voyage there in 1542. During his visits he came into contact with members of the Micmac, Huron and other tribes, and established friendly relations with them. This soon led to the growth of trade in beaver, mink and other furs, which Native Americans caught and sold to Europeans.

Later French explorers began to claim North American land for France. In 1608, Samuel de Champlain founded and claimed Quebec, and in 1682, René Sieur de la Salle declared the whole of the Mississippi River valley a French possession. He called it Louisiana after Louis XIV. By 1700, the French had control of land across much of the North American continent.

ENGLISH COLONISATION

The first English attempts at colonisation of North America were not made until the late 16th century, and it was only in 1606 that the first successful settlement was founded, in Jamestown, Virginia. There, the new arrivals clashed with the local Powhatan tribe and nearly wiped them out in 1644.

Meanwhile in 1620, Puritan settlers known as the Pilgrims had arrived further to the north in what is

THE ARRIVAL OF EUROPEANS

now Massachusetts. They owed their survival to the Wampanoags and other tribes of the region, who taught them how to fish, hunt and grow crops in their new environment. However, as the settlers grew more successful, they tried to take over more land. When the Native Americans resisted, the English attacked the Wampanoag and their allies. Soon the tribe that had once helped the colonists almost ceased to exist. By 1700, the English had colonised most of the east coast.

THE ROAD TO THE RESERVATIONS

By the 19th century, many Native American tribes had been destroyed or forced to adopt European ways of life. However, the Plains tribes in the centre of the country had managed to survive. The introduction of horses and guns by Europeans, and

This painting on buffalo hide was made by members of the Shoshone tribe. It depicts a buffalo dance, a ceremony often carried out immediately before or after a hunt. During the 19th century, both these features of Plains Indian life came to an end following the deliberate slaughter of millions of buffalo (see page 58).

A CLOSER LOOK
Europeans gradually devastated the ancient ways of life of the Native American peoples. As well as killing them in battle, they forced many others from their homelands. They also introduced European diseases such as measles, influenza, tuberculosis and smallpox. The Native Americans had never encountered these diseases before, and had no natural immunity to them. As a result, thousands of Native Americans died.

the arrival of new tribes who had been driven from their original lands, had greatly changed their ways of life. But they still lived by hunting buffalo and maintained many of their old traditions. Then, in mid-century, the situation began to change.

From the late 1840s, increasing numbers of Europeans began to head west, some in search of gold, others wanting land to farm. The territories of the Plains peoples lay on their route. In 1851 the US government adopted a policy of 'concentration'. This meant that each Plains tribe was concentrated in one area, and was not permitted to venture beyond its boundaries. The tribes refused to keep these new rules, but were unable to stop the flood of Europeans who now began to enter their lands.

Soon a long series of wars began between government forces and the Native Americans whose lands they were attempting to take by force. At the same time, the government paid professional hunters to slaughter the buffalo on which the Plains tribes depended. Each year from 1872 to 1874, three million buffalo were killed. In 1876, the Native Americans scored a major victory when they killed General Custer and his troops at the Battle of Little Big Horn. But this was only a reprieve. The end

A CLOSER LOOK

As the colonisers became increasingly greedy for land, more and more Native American tribes were driven from their homelands. Usually the Native Americans were forced on to land that was far less fertile or desirable than their traditional territories. In the 1830s, the American government forced the Southeastern tribes from their territories. Their new 'home' was to be Indian Territory, now the state of Oklahoma, further to the west. The move began in 1831 and, by 1838, the Seminoles, Chickasaw, Choctaw and Creek had made the journey, many dying from hunger and disease on the way. But the Cherokee refused to comply with the government's demands. So government soldiers forced them out and they embarked on what has become known as the 'Trail of Tears'. Of the 13,000 Native Americans who set out, only 9000 arrived at their destination.

THE ARRIVAL OF EUROPEANS

finally came at the Massacre of Wounded Knee on 29 December 1890, when the Dakota leader Big Foot and 200 of his people were slaughtered by American soldiers. As a result, the Native Americans were forced to accept government demands and move to the lands that had been set aside for them, known as reservations.

SPIRIT OF RENEWAL

A young girl in tribal dress at a powwow symbolises the revival of Native American ways of life in the present-day USA.

Since this tragic time, Native Americans have fought hard to regain their freedom and to rebuild their old ways of life. They are beginning to revive their ancient beliefs, skills and languages, and there is even a move to reintroduce buffalo to the Plains.

This spirit of renewal is expressed particularly in the powwow celebrations that are held regularly in many parts of North America. Originally the name given to a tribal meeting accompanied by feasting and present-giving, the term has come to mean a social gathering at which Native Americans from many tribes meet, wear traditional costumes, perform traditional dances and make traditional music.

A CLOSER LOOK

In the USA today, there are over 30 Native American 'tribal' colleges. These colleges teach the skills necessary to be successful in the modern American world as well as ensuring the survival of ancient traditions and skills. Religious ceremonies are practised and languages spoken and taught, allowing Native American culture to flourish.

TIMELINE

c. **60,000 years ago**	Beringia landbridge first emerges.
c. **40,000-12,000 years ago**	Waves of hunters cross from Siberia to Alaska on foot.
c. **40,000-10,000 years ago**	Palaeo-Indian Period

BC

c. **10,000-9200**	Period of the Clovis culture
c. **9000-8000**	Period of the Folsom culture
c. **8000**	Beginning of Archaic Period
c. **1000**	Early settlements of the Adena culture established in the Southeast. Dorset culture arises in the eastern Arctic.

Various dates from

c. **1000**	Beginning of the Woodland Period – Native Americans start to practise agriculture.
c. **300**	Hopewell culture replaces Adena in the Southeast. Hohokam culture emerges in the Southwest.
c. **200**	Basketmakers emerge in the Southwest.

AD

c. **3rd century**	Mogollon culture emerges in the Southwest.
c. **500**	Decline of Hopewell culture begins.
c. **700**	Mississippians emerge in the Southeast. Anasazi emerge in the Southwest.
c. **1000**	Thule culture develops in Alaska. Mogollon begin to live above ground.
c. **1050-1250**	Mississippian town of Cahokia at its height.
c. **1100**	Anasazi begin to build cliffside apartment houses.
c. **1300**	Hohokam begin to construct adobe villages.
14th century	Decline of the Mogollon culture. Anasazi abandon their towns and villages.
c. **1450**	Decline of Mississippians begins. Decline of Hohokam culture begins.
15th century	Apache and Navajo tribes arrive in the Southwest.
1492-1504	Christopher Columbus's four voyages to the Americas.
1534-42	Jacques Cartier makes three voyages to Canada.
1539-42	Hernando de Soto crosses the Southeast.
1540-2	Francisco Vásquez de Coronado crosses the Southwest.
1565	The Spanish colonise Florida.
Late 16th century	Mohawk, Onondaga, Seneca, Oneida and Cayuga tribes form the Iroquois League.
1606	First successful English colony founded in Jamestown, Virginia.
1608	Samuel de Champlain founds Quebec.
1620	Puritan settlers from England arrive in Massachusetts.
1682	René Sieur de la Salle claims the Mississippi River valley for France and names it Louisiana.
18th century	Southeastern Creek tribe move to Florida and become the Seminole.
1840s	Europeans begin to head for the American West in large numbers.
1850s-1890	Wars between Native Americans and forces of the US government
1851	The US government introduces policy of concentration.
1870-83	Extermination of the Plains buffalo herds by professional hunters.
1876	Battle of Little Bighorn.
1890	Massacre of Wounded Knee.

GLOSSARY

adobe – brick made of sun-dried mud.

anthropologist – a person who studies human beings and their ways of life.

archaeologist – a person who studies the past by excavating ancient sites and examining ancient objects.

chickee – an open-sided house of Florida's Seminole tribe.

corral – an enclosed area into which animals are driven for capture.

cradleboard – a lace-up leather pouch with a wooden back in which Native American women carried their babies.

culture area – one of the ten areas into which anthropologists divide North America. The Native American tribes in each area often have similar ways of life.

earth lodge – a sunken, dome-shaped dwelling of earth, wood and grass, inhabited by the farming tribes of the Plains.

earthwork – a large, raised structure made of earth.

gourd – any of several types of fruit with thick, often brightly coloured shells.

hierarchical – arranged in ranks or classes.

hogan – a wood and earth dwelling with a domed roof.

hunter-gatherer – a person who acquires food by hunting animals and gathering plants.

Ice Age – any of several periods of Earth's history during which much of the planet's surface was covered with ice. The most recent Ice Age lasted from about 1.6 million to about 11,000 years ago.

kachina – one of the many spirits recognised by the Pueblo peoples of the Southwest.

kayak – a type of small, wood and sealskin canoe used by Arctic tribes.

kiva – an underground room used for religious rituals by men of the Pueblo peoples.

longhouse – a large, rectangular, wood and bark dwelling with a curved roof inhabited by members of some Northeastern tribes.

mastodon – any of a group of extinct, elephantlike creatures with trunks and tusks.

midden – a rubbish mound.

moccasin – a type of shoe made from soft leather and worn by tribes from several culture areas, including the Subarctic and Northeast.

moiety – one of two groups to which the clans of some Northwestern tribes belonged.

parfleche – a carrying case used by Plains tribes and made by folding buffalo hides into a box or envelope shape.

potlatch – a ceremony held by Northwestern tribes at which large numbers of gifts were distributed by the host.

powwow – a tribal meeting, now often a mainly social event with dancing, music-making etc.

rawhide – hide (animal skin) that has been dehaired but not treated to turn it into leather.

shaman – a man or woman believed to have the ability to contact the spirits and use their power, for example to heal the sick.

stockade – a fence or other barrier made of wooden stakes.

tipi – a tentlike dwelling made of buffalo hides stretched over wooden poles.

totem – any of several spirit animals, such as a bear or an eagle, that each symbolised a different Northwestern clan or moiety.

travois – a triangular wood and buffalo hide frame drawn by a dog or horse and used to transport goods.

tuber – a thick, underground stem.

tundra – the treeless area of permanently frozen ground between the Arctic ice cap and the forested region further south.

umiak – a type of sailing boat made of wood or whalebone covered with walrus hides and used by Arctic tribes.

wampum – valuable shell beads used by Northeastern tribes to create objects such as belts. After the arrival of Europeans, wampum became a form of currency.

wickiup – a cone-shaped dwelling made of wood and brush.

INDEX